BRANCH LINE TO SWANAGE

Vic Mitchell and Keith Smith

First published July 1986
Reprinted April 1989
Revised and reprinted April 1992

Design – Deborah Goodridge

ISBN 0906520 33 9

Published by Middleton Press
Easebourne Lane
Midhurst, West Sussex.
GU29 9AZ
☎ *073 081 3169*

Typeset by CitySet · Bosham 573270

Printed & bound by Biddles Ltd,
Guildford and Kings Lynn.

CONTENTS

ACKNOWLEDGEMENTS

Our thanks go to R. Allen, R. Brasher, D. Cash, D. Haysom, J. Parker, K. Pfrangley, R. Panting, C. Phillips, M. Stollery and J. Walker who are involved in the Swanage Railway Project. We are also indebted to T.M. Junor and J.F. Sharp for information regarding BP. Our gratitude as always must be expressed to Mrs. E. Fisk, R. Randell, N. Stanyon and our wives for assistance in production and also to the many photographers mentioned in the credits who have helped in other ways.

GEOGRAPHICAL SETTING

The Isle of Purbeck is almost an island, bounded on the north by the River Frome and Poole Harbour; on the east and south by the sea, and connected to the mainland by high ground only at its western end. Its unique geology has had an important effect on railway traffic and still does. The southern area consists of Purbeck Beds, a source of good building stone; the central area yielded Purbeck marble and china clay, while the Poole Harbour shoreline is now the site of a number of substantial oil wells. The varied geology has given rise to a spectacular landscape and coastline which has attracted millions of railway passengers over the years.

The geological boundaries run east-west. The first half of the branch runs across infertile heath land before reaching Corfe Castle, situated in a gap in the impressive chalk outcrop of the Purbeck Hills. Their large angle of dip makes them a striking feature. They continue as a submarine ridge to link with the spine of the Isle of Wight at The Needles.

The route then continues on a plain of Wealden Clay to Swanage, soon running parallel to the gently dipping stone-bearing beds to the south.

All maps in this album are to the scale of 25″ to 1 mile, unless otherwise stated.

(Railway Magazine)

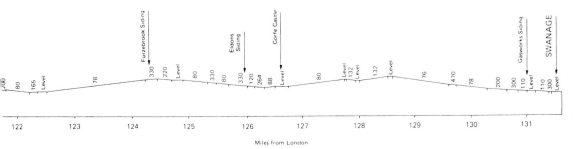

1. Quarrymen Harry Chinchen and Walter Brown are seen working a 'freestone' seam aided only by the light of tallow candles on 10th October 1923. Note the pillared hard stone supporting the high ceiling of this 'lane', unlike many in which the quarrymen were unable to stand upright. Underground workings of this type were largely closed or worked out by World War II. The cheaper more productive method of 'open-cast' stone quarrying took over completely. However, 1982 remarkably saw the re-opening of an old underground quarry by the Bonfield family, as this traditional method has once again proved economical. (W. Powell)

HISTORICAL BACKGROUND

A small station came into use at Wareham when the Southampton and Dorchester line opened on 1st June 1847. This route ran via Wimborne and was unconcerned with the then infant Bournemouth.

A number of proposals were made for a branch to Swanage but it was left to local entrepreneurs led by Mr. George Burt, to initiate the successful scheme. Passenger traffic commenced on 20th May 1885 and goods services on 1st June.

From early in the 19th century, a particularly pure form of china clay had been dug in an area north west of Corfe Castle and had largely been sent away by sea, from piers in Poole Harbour. During pre-history this material (of granite origin) had been transported by rivers from the Dartmoor extrusions and deposited in this localised area.

Another unusual mineral was Purbeck marble, an ornamental stone used to some extent in Victorian church and cathedral work, particularly for interior effects.

Purbeck stone has been quarried (in the open or underground) west of Swanage for generations and was largely exported by sea. To facilitate this, the first standard gauge line in the area was laid from the stone yards on the sea front onto the pier. The initial plan was to link this track direct to the quarries. A later abortive scheme was to join it with the branch from Wareham, when it arrived.

The branch was operated by the London & South Western Railway from the outset and its successor, the Southern Railway, introduced a number of improvements, which will become apparent in the ensuing photographs.

British Railways modernised the rolling stock but eventually closed the branch on 3rd January 1972, although about two miles was retained for mineral traffic.

Preservation proposals were made and after an uphill struggle, the licence to use Swanage station was obtained in 1975. Track re-laying had progressed sufficiently in 1979 for operation over a short length to recommence. Since Easter 1984 trains have run over the one mile of restored track, at weekends and in the holiday season.

PASSENGER SERVICES

The initial frequency was five return journeys a day and this was increased to six by 1890. By 1910 there were ten trips on weekdays and two on Sundays, this service being increased by 50% by 1922.

The weekday service in the summer of 1938 comprised 17 trains each way, of which one was a Waterloo through train with restaurant car. There were three such trains additionally on Saturdays. On Sundays eleven trips were made.

A reduced service of about nine weekday and four Sunday trains was run during World War II, but the post-war timetable was similar to that operated in the late 1930s.

Through running, other than to Waterloo, was infrequent – Bournemouth being the principal destination, although an early morning departure from Broadstone was shown for many years.

The DEMU service from October 1967 to the end gave eleven trips on weekday and nine on Sundays, although the latter was provided by road in the winters. Other less common workings are described in some of the captions.

PIER TRAMWAY

The Swanage Pier Tramway was designed by Capt. W.S. Moorsom, the Chief Engineer of the Southampton & Dorchester Railway, who on visiting Swanage was astonished at the archaic manner in which stone was loaded by hand onto ships in the bay. He believed that those involved in the stone trade seemed totally unaware of modern improvements and unless they roused themselves he saw no reason why the trade should not die out altogether.

Consequently, prominent local citizens formed the Swanage Pier & Tramway Co. with John Mowlem as its chairman and among the directors, his nephew George Burt; both of whom were to have an important influence on bringing the railway to Swanage. The Swanage Pier & Tramway Act received royal assent on 8th August 1859 giving consent for a Pier at Swanage and "a tramway to connect the stone quarries in the parishes of Langton Matravers and Swanage with such pier or jetty". This would have involved the construction of about four miles of standard gauge railway with the intention of joining with the LSWR, should a line be built from Wareham. Due to the gradients existing, certain branches from the main tramway would be required at Langton, probably worked by gravity.

Only the initial section of the tramway was constructed for approximately ⅓ mile from the pier to the 'bankers' or stone-yards on the sea front, where the Parade now stands. This was due to the opposition from local residents and land owners in Swanage, yet the quarrymen themselves were eager to have the line continued.

No locomotives, stationary or otherwise, were permitted under the 1859 Act in the vicinity of houses in Swanage. Consequently single or teams of horses were used to move the loaded wagons. However, little stone was carried by the new tramway as the pier itself was structurally unsound and frequently criticised in the local newspapers when easterly gales regularly broke away large sections. The stone merchants continued to load stone in the traditional way, which involved man-handling the stone up to five times before it was ready to be taken by the stone barges to London or beyond. The fact that the tramway never reached the quarries also influenced their thinking and it was only the coming of the railway in 1885 and the desire to develop the sea-front as part of the tourist resort which forced the merchants to move their 'bankers' to the new station site.

The main cargoes handled by the tramway were coal, timber and fish, with two large cranes on the pier to assist loading and unloading. These were were later removed as the number of paddle steamers plying between Bournemouth and Swanage increased. A coal and fish store was built at the town end of the tramway in the late 1880s, when the merchants moved their yards to the station. The store was also used as a morgue for the bodies of shipwreck victims.

The rapidly growing holiday trade led eventually to the building of a new pleasure pier in 1896. As a consequence, the tramway which had previously dominated the pier with two standard gauge lines was altered to one single line for the part used by the holiday visitors and re-gauged throughout to 2′6″. The old pier continued to be used by fishermen and for coaling-up the paddle steamers until the outbreak of World War I. Isolated sections of the tramway were used during the 1920s although, by the early thirties, only one wagon remained.

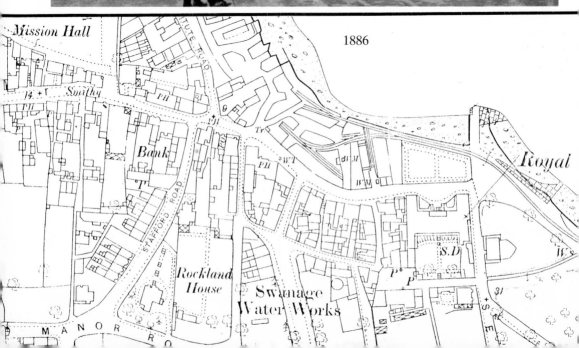

1886

2. On the right is the high-wheeled wagon from which the stone was transferred into a stone-boat (or 'lighter'), each carrying up to nine tons. It was then rowed out to the sailing ketch, in this photograph the *Brisk*, anchored in the bay onto which the stone was hoisted. This seemingly archaic system remained in use until the railway came in 1885, despite the fact that the original Pier (of which a few timber piles survive next to the "new" Pier) had been built over twenty-five years earlier. (W. Pouncy/D. Haysom collection)

3. The location of this banker on the 1886 map is indicated by the bridge. Some stone troughs are in the foreground and some wagons stand to the right of the crane. (J. Ward collection)

4. A trio of paddle steamers – left to right, *The Premier, Balmoral* and *Monarch* – are being coaled by hand from Pier Tramway trucks in about 1910. This practice ceased with the advent of World War I. (J. Ward collection)

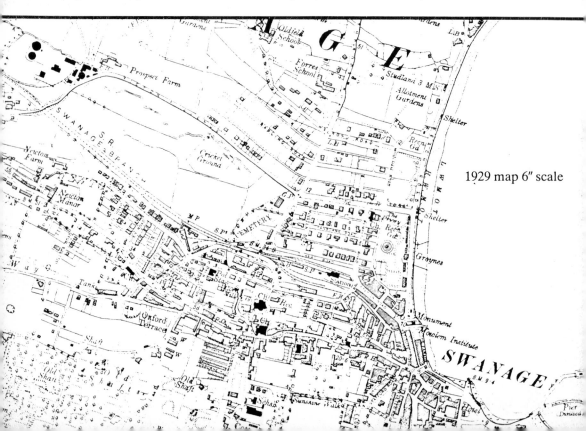

1929 map 6" scale

5. A photograph from about 1890 shows the tramway curving off the pier along the foreshore and then turning inland. (D. Haysom collection)

6. Most of the land-based track and some points were set into concrete and remain visible today as an important relic of the town's history. This 1968 view shows, on the left, the wall of an amusement arcade which was earlier a coal and fish store. (D. Cullum)

7. The elegant 0415 class was designed by Adams for outer suburban work and they eventually found more rural pastures, the last examples being found on the Lyme Regis branch. (D. Cullum collection)

1885

Wareham to Swanage.					
Wareham ..	8 30	11 10	3 40	5 50	9 10
Corfe Castle.	8 43	11 23	3 53	6 3	9 25
Swanage ..	8 53	11 33	4 3	6 13	9 40
Swanage to Wareham.					
Swanage ..	7 20	10 15	2 30	5 5	6 35
Corfe Castle.	7 31	10 25	2 40	5 15	6 47
Wareham ..	7 45	10 40	2 53	5 28	7 2

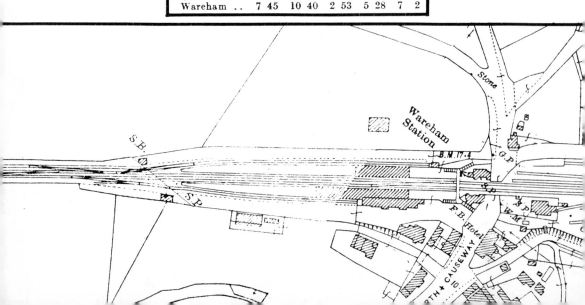

8. Another view in LSWR days shows no. 375 westbound, with an octagonal gas lantern on the platform, not the common square ones seen in the previous photograph. (D. Cullum collection)

1909

Mls.			mrn	mrn	mrn	mrn	mrn	aft	aft	aft	aft	aft	THURS.	g		SUNDAYS. aft	aft
	Wareham	.. dep.	8 18	10 0	11 48	1 25	3 20	4 6	4 55	5 44	6 50	8 15		11 50 ..	3 47	9 13 ..
6	Corfe Castle	.. ..	8 31	10 13	12 1	1 38	3 33	4 19	5 8	5 57	7 ?	8 28		12 4 —	4 0	9 26 ..
11	Swanage ..	.. arr.	8 42	10 24	12 12	1 49	3 44	4 33	5 20	6 12	7 14	8 39		12 14 ..	4 11	9 37 ..

Mls.			mrn	mrn	mrn	mrn	aft	aft	aft	aft	aft	aft	THURS.	b		SUNDAYS. aft	aft
..	Swanage ..	.. dep.	7 40	7 58	9 5	10 50	12 43	2 57	4 10	4 58	5 50	7 35		9 45 ..	2 45	5 45 ..
5	Corfe Castle	.. ..	7 52	8 9	9 17	11 2	12 55	3 9	4 22	5 11	6 3	7 47		9 57 ..	2 57	5 57 ..
11	Wareham	.. arr.	8 4	8 20	9 29	11 14	1 7	3 21	4 34	5 23	6 15	7 59		10 10 ..	3 9	6 9 ..

b Runs to Bournemouth West.   g From Bournemouth West.

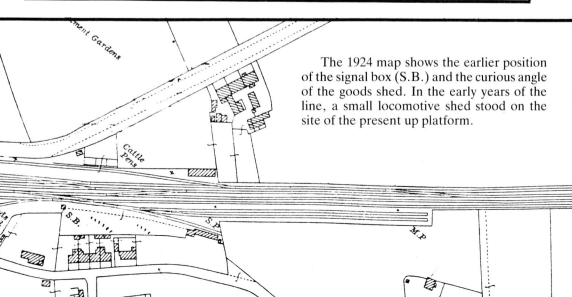

The 1924 map shows the earlier position of the signal box (S.B.) and the curious angle of the goods shed. In the early years of the line, a small locomotive shed stood on the site of the present up platform.

9. A locomotive class that served the branch for over 30 years was the M7 0–4–4T. Here no. 30108 stands in the up bay whilst no. 30128 waits on the down main line. The train it is propelling is probably bound for Swanage, being one of the few to originate from Bournemouth. (F.W. Ivey)

10. Until the advent of BR Standard locomotives, the branch was largely worked by push-pull units. Set no. 606 is stabled at the end of the up siding, close to the up home signals west of the station. Although built in the 1930s, the driving controls and end windows were not fitted until the mid-1950s. (J. Scrace)

11. Two coaches have been detached from a down Waterloo train on 14th July 1960 and the branch line locomotive is about to haul them to Swanage whilst propelling the branch coaches. (H.C. Casserley)

12. "Change for the Swanage branch" was the call from the platform staff, as class 5 no. 73041 arrived with the 2.55pm from Bournemouth Central on 8th June 1964. The 3.37 to Swanage is standing on the site of the present car park. (J. Scrace)

13. Those who remember the last years of steam on the branch will cherish this view in their memory – maybe having enjoyed it from one of the garden-style seats on the platform. This is another photograph from June 1964. (J. Scrace)

(7/49)

SOUTHERN
BRITISH RAILWAYS
REGION

Stock
787

TO

WAREHAM

14. There were three trailing crossovers under the control of the signal box, this one being the middle one. Swanage branch trains usually arrived at platform 4 and departed from platform 1. (D. Cullum)

15. At the east end of the platforms there was a charming pair of crossing keeper's cottages and, on the up platform, other long lost features include the ticket collector's shelter and the inspector's office. (D. Cullum)

16. No.29 gatehouse was on the up side and probably dated from the opening of the line. One of two foot crossings now passes over its site. (D. Cullum)

18. The crew admire no. 35029 *Ellerman Lines* on an up Channel Island boat train in August 1966 – the guard from his doorway; the fireman from the tank top, whilst the driver stands at ease. The white diamond on the signal post indicated track circuiting in use. Hundreds now gaze at this engine in York Railway Museum, where it is shown with its firebox and boiler sectioned. (J.H. Bird)

17. Looking east from the footbridge in 1965, we see the station master's house which was adjacent to the first station. Beyond it is the goods shed which, together with the signal box, survived intact in 1986. The former was erected in 1847 and the latter in 1928. One LSWR gate remained in use but all have now gone, replaced by a road bridge to the east. (D. Cullum)

19. Empty clay wagons rattle past the "down starter" behind class 4 4–6–0 no. 75075 on 21st June 1967. This SR pattern signal was built from two old running rails whilst the "bay starter" was of the LSWR lattice construction. Steam traction ended in 1967 but the water tank remained until 1972.
(G.M. Moon)

Other photographs and maps of this station and Worgret Junction can be seen in our *Bournemouth to Weymouth* album.

20. Examples of the replacement motive power are seen on 7th August 1969 in the form of no. D6529 on the 12.30 from Waterloo and DEMU no. 1128 on the 14.41 to Swanage. (J. Scrace)

21. A storm cloud on 3rd May 1986 silhouettes the 1980 road bridge, while the sun still shines on oil tankers in the down sidings and on insulators in the "six-foot". Electrified services commenced on 16th May 1988, by which time the pedestrian crossing was light controlled. The former goods shed (right) was at an unusual angle to the main line. A similar arrangement existed at Ringwood and is illustrated in *Branch Lines around Wimborne*.
(V.Mitchell)

WORGRET JUNCTION

22. Local objectors insisted on the junction being so far west of the town, which can be seen in the distance in this view taken from under the A352 road bridge. Standard class 4 tank no. 80147 slows down for the junction on 8th June 1964. (J. Scrace)

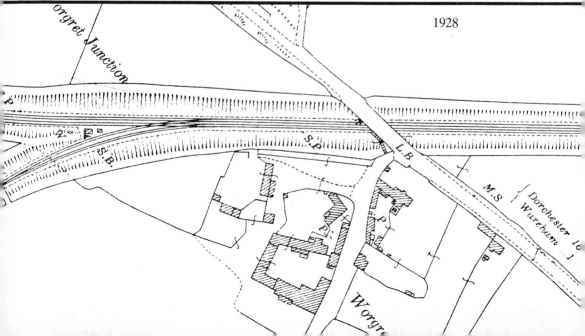

1928

23. Viewed from the road bridge it is evident that up trains from the branch only worked "wrong line" for a few yards. Since the aboli-tion of the signal box on 23rd May 1976, mineral trains from the branch work wrong line for over a mile to Wareham. (D. Cullum)

24. A pleasant sight from the signal box on 13th July 1963 as class M7 no. 30667 takes the curve with the 12.14 from Wareham. (E. Wilmshurst)

25. A few minutes later, sister engine no. 30108 passes the box with the 12.14 from Swanage. Today, only an exposed 5-lever ground frame stands at the junction. (E. Wilmshurst)

27. In the last year of steam, main line passenger locomotives were sometimes relegated to local freight work. This example is no. 34018 *Axminster*, devoid of nameplates, crossing Stoborough Heath and bound for Furzebrook siding, with empty china clay wagons. (S.C. Nash)

26. The signalman stands by the tablet catcher on 23rd March 1967 as a MRTS railtour enters the branch, hauled by class 2 no. 41320. The line crosses the River Frome ½ mile south of the junction and south of that again it traverses the open ground of Stoborough Heath. (J.H. Bird)

FURZEBROOK

28. On the south side of the branch, an exchange siding was provided with the 2′8½″ gauge lines of Pike Bros., large producers of china clay. M7 no. 30106 propels empty wagons into the siding whilst its loaded train stands in the loop, on 12th June 1952. (S.W. Baker)

29. No. 34025 *Whimple* rests in the loop on 30th June 1967 on the last steam rostered working. The gate to the private siding is visible, but the ground frame seen in the last picture had gone by then. (G.M. Moon)

30. On the north side of the branch, sidings were laid in 1978 for the loading of crude oil from the Wytch Farm oilfield. The oil was conveyed by a three mile pipeline from the wells, which are on the shore of Poole Harbour. The clay transhipment shed is the smaller building on the left, its siding being visible in the gap in the hedge. Clay traffic ceased in 1982 but was resumed in July 1986 when 57-ton capacity bogie wagons were despatched on most working days to Stoke-on-Trent, although only one or two at a time. The traffic ceased again in March 1992 as a result of the Government's fragmentation of the railway system and despite its declared policy of transferring freight from road to rail.

From 1979 until 1990, there were normally two oil trains daily to Llandarcy Refinery. As a result of drilling deeper wells in the late 1980s, the output of the oilfield was increased about ten-fold. This necessitated an oil pipe line to Fawley Refinery but the railway was still required to carry liquified petroleum gases, which had previously been despatched by road in small quantities. The tanks on the right were removed, an additional long siding was laid between the two illustrated above and new loading and compressing equipment was installed. Block trains commenced running on 20th November 1990, their destination being Avonmouth, from where the gas is exported, notably to Spain. (British Petroleum)

31a. Associated with the oil are three gases - methane, which is piped into the gas grid, butane which is loaded at the siding on the left, and propane, the tankers for which are seen in the centre road. The rail borne gases are carried as liquids under pressure - LPG. The siding on the right is intended for crippled wagons but is seldom used. (V.Mitchell)

31b. This and the previous photograph were taken on 22nd February, when no. 60051 hauled a train of 1189 tons gross weight, carrying 250 tons of butane and 230 tons of propane in 29 tankers. It is seen on the points to the loading compound and adjacent to the headshunt of goods loop seen in picture 30. At that time, seven to nine trains of LPG were loaded each week, as part of a 15 year contract. (V.Mitchell)

PIKE BROS. RAILWAY

China clay working on the northern slopes of the Purbeck Hills commenced in the early nineteenth century and in the early 1860s a 2′8½″ gauge railway of about 5 route miles was laid down to a wharf on the River Frome at Ridge, about a mile south-east of Wareham. In 1884, this line was bisected by the Swanage branch at Furzebrook, where an exchange siding was provided.

From the onset of World War II, the line to Ridge Wharf ceased to be used as Middlebere Heath was requisitioned by the Army for training purposes.

Several clay pits and mines were served by the railway together with large areas of weathering grounds, where the clay was unloaded and allowed to stand in lumps or balls for 6 months or so. This gave rise to the term "ball clay", which is still used although the practice has ceased, having been replaced by modern processing methods.

Pike Bros. amalgamated in 1949 with B. Fayle & Co., the other large Purbeck firm winning china clay. The railway systems, although only a mile apart, were never linked, being of different gauges.

The last mine to be rail served was Grange Mine, in 1956, and their railway operation ceased entirely the following year.

The merged companies became part of English China Clays (ECC) in 1968 and continued to despatch their products by BR from the Furzebrook siding, until 1982.

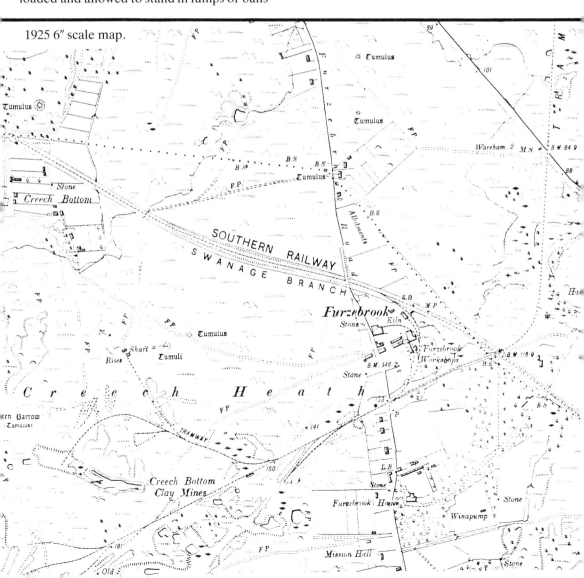

1925 6″ scale map.

32. This is the other end of the tranship shed, seen in photographs 28 and 29. *Secundus*, an 0–6–0WT, is seen shunting loaded clay wagons on 22nd May 1953. (S.W. Baker)

34. *Secundus* waits with a train of side-tipping empties as a Simplex passes by with a couple of well loaded wagons, between which a pair of legs project. An open truck was provided for workmen to travel in and was called the Jury Car. (S.W. Baker)

←

33. 0–4–2ST *Septimus*, built by Peckett in 1930, stands in the sun in June 1951. One of the two locomotive sheds is on the right and the wagon shop on the left, with the curved roof. The company operated about 150 wagons in 1938. (S.W. Baker)

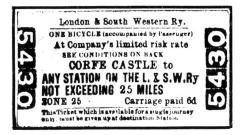

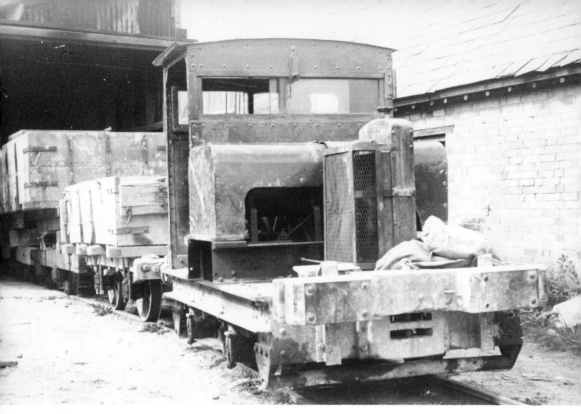

35. The Simplex was produced in large quantities during World War I and many were used in France to supply the battlefront. After the war, many industrial concerns bought "Govt Surplus" examples, many of which retained armour plating for many years. (S.W. Baker)

36. 0–6–0ST *Tertius* was supplied by Manning Wardle in 1886 and is seen outside the Furzebrook shed, after having been rebuilt in 1951 with this high-pitched boiler. A second locomotive shed had earlier been in use at Ridge. (S.W. Baker)

37. *Secundus* was purchased from Belliss & Seekings and arrived in May 1874. When photographed being oiled up in May 1953, it was kept as a spare engine and was on its fourth boiler. This 9-ton 0–6–0ST had disc wheels and wooden brake blocks. It can be seen today in the Birmingham Museum. (S.W. Baker)

38. *Quintus* was an 0–4–0ST built in 1914 by Manning Wardle and is seen here at East Creech, about a mile from the exchange sidings. Short drivers were an advantage on some narrow gauge locomotives. (S.W. Baker)

40. Clay was both mined and quarried. This is Greenspecks Mine in 1952 where the 18″ gauge mine wagons, on the left, were discharged into 2′8½″ gauge trucks. One of the former type is exhibited at the Chalk Pits Museum in West Sussex. (S.W. Baker)

←

39. The originators of the use of latin names for the fleet had not anticipated six locomotives. *Sextus* was the penultimate, arriving in 1925 from Peckett with *Septimus* following in 1930, from the same builder. (S.W. Baker)

←

41. B. Fayle & Co. had their exchange siding a little to the north of the Corfe Castle down distant signal. The tipper wagon on the right indicates the position of the 2ft. gauge track, in August 1966. During World War II, the Army had a siding on the west side of the track, near the tranship shed, and two more curved ones, further north on the east side, for use by massive rail-mounted guns. The former was usable from November 1941 until June 1946 and the latter from November 1940 until the summer of 1946. (D. Cullum)

42. Looking south to Nine Barrow Down on 18th June 1967, we can witness the return of the RCTS Railtour, with a locomotive at each end. Special trains had run in this manner before. For example, on one hectic Saturday in 1944 (17th June), four such specials were run on the branch, in connection with the invasion of Europe. (J. Scrace)

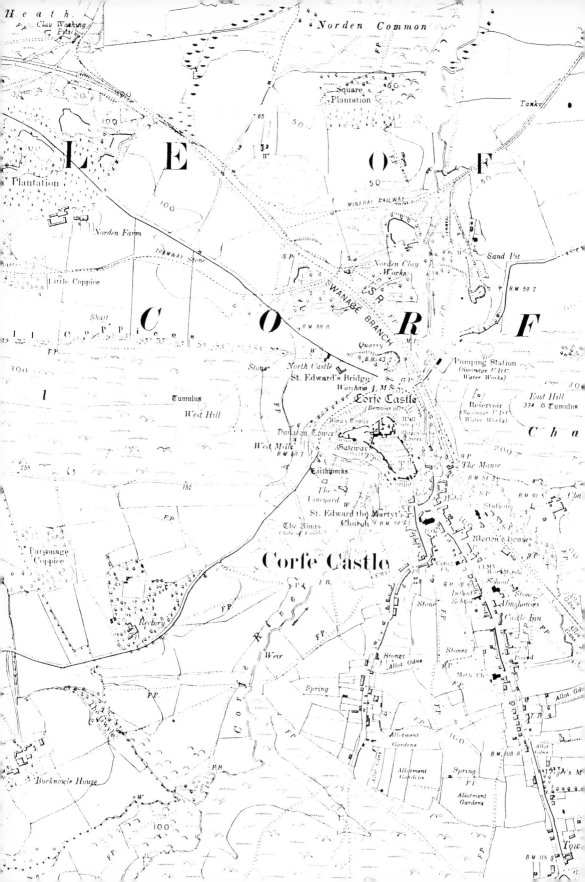

FAYLE'S TRAMWAY

This was the popular name of the line sometimes known as the Goathorn Railway, after the pier on Poole Harbour where it terminated until about 1936. There had earlier been another pier near Middlebere Farm, close to better known Wytch Farm, where clay had also been unloaded into small vessels. These sailed to Poole where the cargo was loaded onto sea-going ships.

The railway was laid to the unusual gauge of 3′9″ and the first locomotive was built in 1870 by Stephen Lewin of Poole, who might be described as a railway enthusiast of some stature. It was named *Tiny* and was joined by only one other locomotive, *Thames*, another 0–4–0ST. This was acquired in 1905, second-hand.

After World War II, replacement rolling stock of that gauge was unobtainable and so it was decided to re-gauge the remaining line to 1′11½″. The locomotives are illustrated in the following pages. Their usage declined and finally ceased in 1972.

6″ scale map of 1929. The Transhipment siding on this scale is not clear, but is above the large **E**. The siding was known as Eldon's, after Lord Eldon, a local landowner.

43. The only known passenger service on the line was provided in 1934-36 for the ten children of clay workers who lived in the Goathorn area and attended school in Corfe Castle. The education authority paid the company 7s 6d (37½p) per day for the service. The locomotive is *Thames*, built by Manning Wardle in 1902. (S.P.W. Corbett)

SOUTHERN RAILWAY

SWANAGE BRANCH

W

Stone

A351

WAY

S.P

The 1928 map shows the exchange sidings in the top left-hand corner.

MINERAL RAILWAY

TRAMWAY

Norden Clay Works

Corfe River

W.M.

F.P.

44. A general view of Norden pit in 1952 reveals the method of working and how the clay starts its rail journey. In more than one case, steam for the winch that hauled the wagons up the incline was provided by the boiler of a retired locomotive (S.W. Baker)

45. A closer look at ball clay production shows a pneumatic spade in use on the left. Compressed air for this was delivered through the black pipe seen running across the middle of the previous picture. (S.W. Baker)

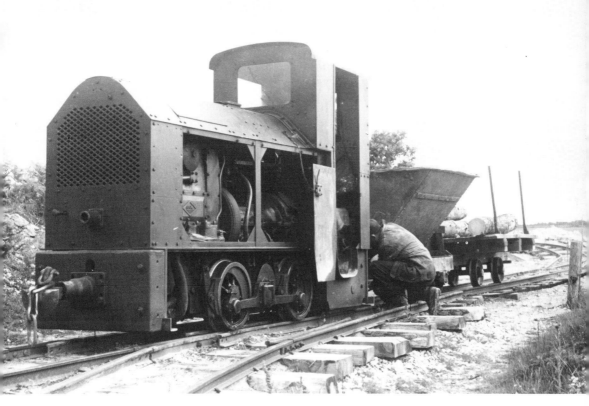

47. The other diesel locomotive was built by Orenstein & Koppel (works no. 20777) and is reputed to have previously worked on a German V2 rocket site. (S.W. Baker)

←

46. After the regauging to "2ft", three diesel and one steam locomotive were purchased. This is one of the two Simplex diesels (works no. 179889) and is seen pushing wagons of clay, ready for despatch, over the weighbridge in June 1952. (S.W. Baker)

48. The steamer was the now famous 2–6–2T *Russell*, built for the North Wales Narrow Gauge Railway in 1906 by Hunslet. This line was extended to become the Welsh Highland Railway, which was eventually controlled by the Festiniog Railway. This latter company reduced the height of *Russell* in an unsuccessful attempt to make it pass through their tunnels – hence the odd shaped doorway, partly in the roof. It was sold to the Hook Norton Ironworks in 1941 from where it was purchased for clay haulage. It is seen here on 22nd May 1953, running as an 0–6–2T (the leading wheels are in the foreground). In 1954, a successful appeal for £140 was made to cover the cost of its purchase and transport to the infant Narrow Gauge Railway Museum at Towyn in Wales. Since that time, extensive repairs have been carried out at a number of different locations and it is now back in Wales again with the prospect of steaming again on a short part of the Welsh Highland Railway. (S.W. Baker)

49. Later the same day, we see *Russell* crossing the Wareham-Swanage main road, protected by the traditional red flag. The train would then cross the BR line on an overbridge to reach the weathering grounds. (S.W. Baker)

50. An August 1966 view reveals neglected structures and poor track but gives us our first sight of the castle. The BR line is largely hidden from view by bracken. (D. Cullum)

NORTH OF
CORFE CASTLE

51. With Wytch Heath and Poole Harbour in the background, M7 no. 30060 struggles up the 1 in 88 bank with the two branch coaches, plus four from Waterloo, on 23rd August 1958. The strata being almost end on here, the geology changes rapidly – there is a chalk quarry on the left and a sand pit on the right of centre. (S.C. Nash)

Overleaf →

52. The varied scenery reached its most impressive form as the line approached Corfe Castle to cross the chalk spine of the Isle of Purbeck. The natural mound on which the Norman castle was built is within the Corfe River Gap. No. 30318 drifts north with a train of empties on 4th April 1953. (S.W. Baker)

→

54. The four-arched Purbeck stone viaduct carries the line over the road to Studland and the Corfe River passes through the adjacent arch, on its way north to Poole Harbour. A rake of empty coal wagons rattle past on 17th June 1957, behind Q class no. 30541. Swanage must have consumed a lot of coal that summer. (S.C. Nash)

53. Sister M7 propels its ageing coaches through the beautiful downland in the hot August of 1958. The driver rests his arm on the open droplight whilst the fireman enjoys the view. (S.C. Nash)

CORFE CASTLE

55. This well known photograph is reproduced in large form so that we can enjoy many details that can otherwise be easily missed. Below Corfe Castle is the goods shed, with its ornate valance which once sheltered loading carts; the end-loading dock, used by the carriages of the gentry in a bygone age; the elegant row of oil lights; the up local train; the majesty of an L11 and a T9 together and the graceful LSWR signal, topped by a fine finial. The train was a "Sightseeing Tour" from Waterloo in 1935 – out via Southampton and return via Salisbury, using the single line spur from Hamworthy Junction. The fare was 10s 6d (52½p) – good value, even in those days. (Dr. I.C. Allen)

London & South Western Ry.
This Ticket is issued subject to the Regulations
& Conditions stated in the Company's Time
Tables & Bills
WOOL to
CORFE CASTLE
Via Wareham
Wool   Wool
Corfe Castle   (S.1)   Corfe Castle
3rd CLASS   **3rd CLASS**
Fare 11d   Fare 11d

London & South Western Ry.
ONE DOG
Accompanied by passenger
CORFE CASTLE to
ANY STATION ON THE L. & S. W. Ry
NOT EXCEEDING   10 MILES
FOR CONDITIONS SEE BACK
Zone **10**   Rate 3d

56. This southward view shows us the only means by which passengers could cross the lines and it also shows sanitary students the size of the well-ventilated "gentlemens" on the up platform. (D. Cullum collection)

57. Lengthy skirts and baggy trousers will help those who can remember them to date this photograph. The ridge tiles of alternating size and the complex barge boards add architectural interest. In 1986, the building was in use by an electronics company. (Lens of Sutton)

58. A view from East Hill shows almost the full length of the station approach road and the good relationship of the station to the village centre. The railway line formed the eastern boundary to the village. (S.W. Baker)

This 1928 layout subsequently changed very little. The point to the west of the goods shed was removed in about 1940 to create two independent sidings.

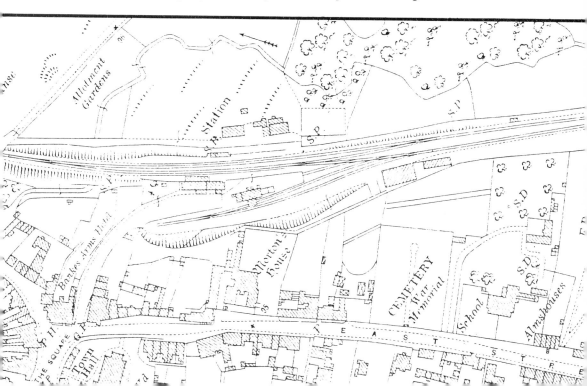

59. The classical viewpoint from which to photograph a down train arriving. This one is an excursion from Waterloo on 6th April 1953, headed by Q class 0–6–0 no. 30458 (S.W. Baker)

60. For many years the camping coach was no. 21, ex-LSWR 3rd class brake no. 2753. It is seen here in 1955, close to the goods yard gates. (J.H. Aston)

61. The signal box was on the down platform and backed onto East Hill. Its front was unusually lacking in windows. It was photo-graphed in September 1955, the year before its function was transferred to an extension of the porters' room, on the opposite platform.

62. U class no. 31806 with the 9.15am from Basingstoke on 6th September 1955 is seen passing the 11.36 up service from Swanage. This locomotive is now preserved on the Mid-Hants Railway. The passing loop had been lengthened at this point in December 1943, in readiness for the D-Day troop move-ments. (J.H. Aston)

63. This lifeless view is included to show the extension of the porters' room that was built (in Purbeck stone) to house a 12-lever frame, which replaced the signal box on the opposite platform on 17th June 1956. (Lens of Sutton)

64. The fine south facade remains little altered today. This 1963 view shows (from L to R) the gents; the ladies room; the booking hall (with dummy dormer) and finally the spacious 4-bedroomed station master's house, complete with bay window. (C.L. Caddy)

65. The much photographed no. 30108 is
seen here on 13th July 1963, ten months
before the faithful M7s left the branch for
good. The fireman wields his coal hammer
whilst the porter/signalman goes to work the
single line apparatus. (E. Wilmshurst)

Adjusted traffic figures for 1953

Passengers – local journeys		131494
Passengers to branch		102646
Passengers from branch		101444
Holiday runabouts		1320

	From branch	To branch
Parcels	9939	28711
Coal	–	11976 tons
Goods	60425 tons	2472 tons

66. Looking towards Swanage in August 1966, the overgrown shunting neck is apparent along with the redundant loading gauge. The goods yard closed on 22nd November 1965 but it continues to be used by L.G. Stockley, the local coal merchants. (D. Cullum)

68. Class 4 2–6–4T no. 80134 arrives with an up train on 3rd September 1966 whilst class 2 2–6–2T waits in the loop. At busy times, light engines were often attached to scheduled trains to reduce line occupation.
(C.L. Caddy)

67. The train is the 11.20 Swanage to Waterloo on 6th August 1966. The Pullman car *Coral* replaced the LSWR coach in 1960. It was joined by *Milan* in 1961 but both were broken up in 1968 when BR decided that Holiday Coaches were uneconomic.
(E. Wilmshurst)

1890

WAREHAM and SWANAGE.—London and South Western.														
Waterloo Station,	mrn	mrn	mrn	mrn	aft	aft	Mls		mrn	mrn	aft	aft	aft	aft
LONDON 44..dep	....	5 50	S	5.11	15 2 20	3 10	....	—	Swanage ....dep	7 30	10 15	12 30	2 30	5 0	6 35
Wareham......dep	8 30	11 23	1 20	3 40	5 53	7 35	....	5	Corfe Castle.........	7 42	10 27	12 42	2 42	5 13	6 47
Corfe Castle	8 45	11 35	1 34	3 55	6 8	7 50	....	11	Wareham 45, 44.arr	7 57	10 42	12 57	2 57	5 28	7 2
Swanage ....arr	8 57	11 50	1 47	4 7	6 20	8 2	....	13¼	WATERLOO 45.arr	12 15	2 20	4 35	7 40	9 50	....

69. The *Dorset Coast Express* was a popular LCGB railtour which took place on 7th May 1967. It was hauled by no. 34023 *Blackmoor Vale* (now on the Bluebell Railway), with class 4 tank no. 80011 at the rear. (J.H. Bird)

70. No. 80011 is seen at the head of the train on its return journey that day. (D. Fereday Glenn)

71. As seen in the lower cover picture, class T9 no. 120 was the first steam locomotive to pass through the station for about 25 years. In the distance, a trolley stands on the end of the track on 10th May 1991. Track laying on the viaduct was completed on 1st March 1992, as plans were made for this engine to have its last steaming on the line on 26th April, prior to returning to the National Railway Museum. Also planned for that date was the first steaming of the rebuilt class M7 no. 245, resulting in two Drummond - designed engines from the 1890s in action on the Middleton Press Weekend on the line. (A.M.P.Wright)

SWANAGE (LSWR)

72. The station is on the right of this 1885 photograph, taken from what is now Station Road and looking north-westwards. The stream now runs below the shops on the south side of this road. On the left is the brewery and house, owned by James Panton.

The embankment behind the fisherman was being built to extend the long siding shown on the 1886 map. As mentioned at the beginning of this album, it was intended to connect this line with the tracks of the Pier Tramway. (W. Pouncy/D. Haysom collection)

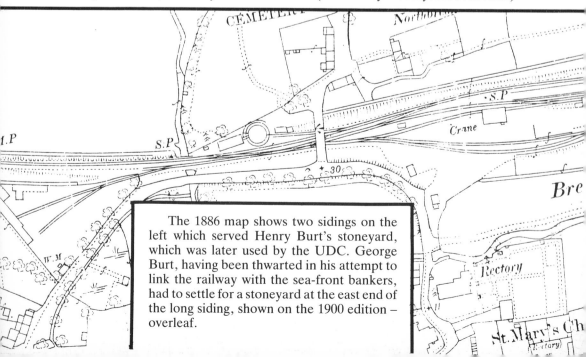

The 1886 map shows two sidings on the left which served Henry Burt's stoneyard, which was later used by the UDC. George Burt, having been thwarted in his attempt to link the railway with the sea-front bankers, had to settle for a stoneyard at the east end of the long siding, shown on the 1900 edition – overleaf.

73. This photograph is still thought by many to be the first passenger train on 20th May 1885. This occasion was in fact greeted with considerable local rejoicing, with many local dignitaries present at the station. However, only the staff are in evidence suitably posed for the local photographer, Thomas Powell. The actual date is thought to be 1887 as the locomotive, Beattie well-tank no.209, was rebuilt with a tender in October of that year and the type of van on the right was probably not introduced until 1887.
(D. Haysom collection)

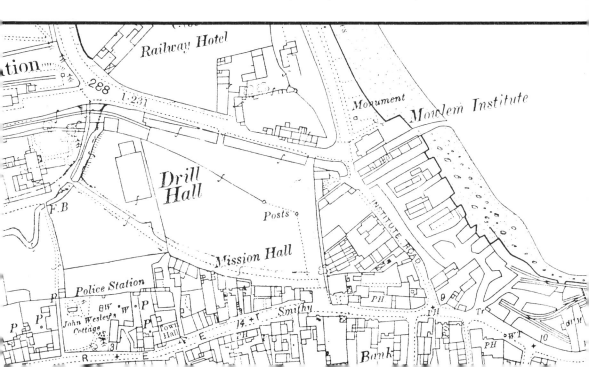

74. The church tower presented an excellent view point for both the goods yard and Swanage Bay. The signal box is on the left; the station on the right and the goods shed is seen in the centre, before its extension in 1897. (F. Frith & Co.)

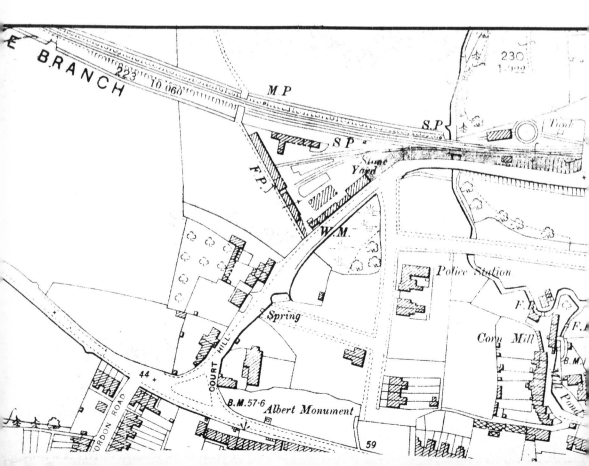

75. A quick photograph before departure, in about 1895, with all heads covered and no teeth visible. (D. Haysom collection)

→

76. Mr. George Parsons was station master from 1885 until 1903 and is seen here with a guard in about 1902. Guards were abolished on push-pull trains of three coaches or less as from 16th October 1933.
(T. Powell/D. Haysom collection)

1900 edition

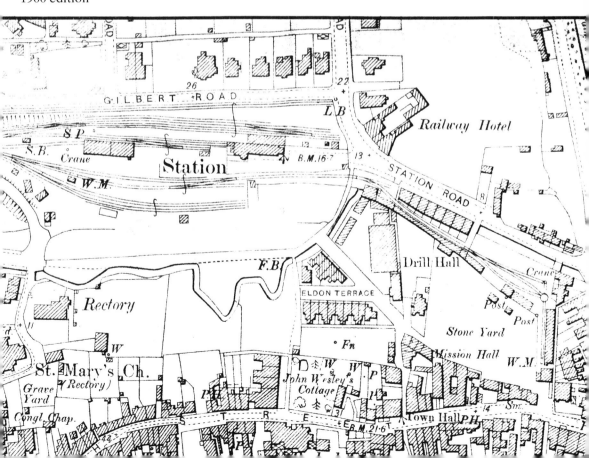

77. Having completed your railway journey, in about 1910, this transport awaited you in the station yard. (D. Haysom collection)

80. Porter George Mayo displays his warm, if not well pressed, LSWR uniform in about 1918, in front of one of the company's vans. (D. Haysom collection)

78. Troops gather during World War I ready for departure, complete with the bandsmen's instruments. The railway station once reflected almost every aspect of community life. (D. Haysom collection)

79. On the same occasion, horses and limbers assemble in the station approach, in readiness for loading onto special trains. Although a much battered photograph, it does record a chapter in the history of the station. (D. Haysom collection)

81. A door swings open and porters hover for a passenger requiring their services, as a train arrives with its distinctive LSWR head-code. The loop at the platform was not provided until November 1897. (Lens of Sutton)

82. Another LSWR view shows no.426, one of the well proportioned 4–4–2Ts designed by William Adams, passing the locomotive shed in July 1921. (H.C. Casserley collection)

SWANAGE (SR)

83. This is still a typical LSWR scene, although taken on 22nd September 1924, nearly two years after the formation of the SR. The 0–4–4T of class T1 still has its Adams-style stovepipe chimney. (Lens of Sutton)

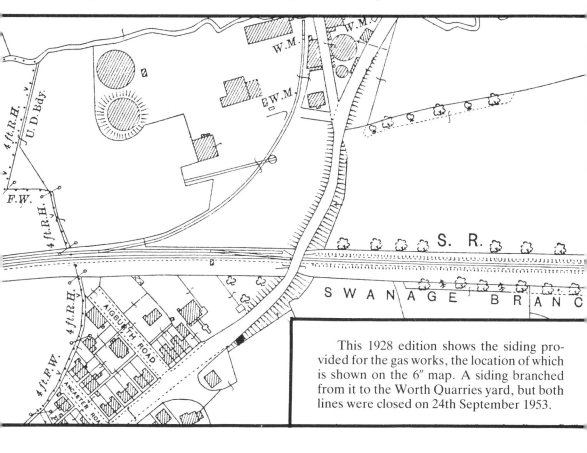

This 1928 edition shows the siding provided for the gas works, the location of which is shown on the 6″ map. A siding branched from it to the Worth Quarries yard, but both lines were closed on 24th September 1953.

84. Class T6 no.E677, with its lengthy tender, was a tight fit on the 50ft turntable on 13th September 1926. The down home signal in the background had a ringed arm under it for access to the goods yard. This was altered on 1st July 1934 to allow passenger trains to officially arrive at the bay. Henry Burt's stoneyard is on the left of this view. (Late E. Wallis)

85. Panton's Brewery was acquired by Strong & Co in 1893 who sold the land and premises to the LSWR in 1899 for the expansion of their goods yard. The two additional sidings on the right were laid down soon after and, in about 1906, the siding across Kings Road to the stoneyard was removed. Date – 13th September 1926. (Late E. Wallis)

```
                    AUGUST BANK HOLIDAY - 1933.

          DOWN TRAINS.          Arrl.              UP TRAINS.            Dep.
                              due pltfm                                 pltfm
  8.33 am Wareham        8.44 Main       7.30 am to Wareham            Main
  8.25 am Bmo West       9.30 Main       8.58 am        "             Main
  9.34 am Wareham        9.57 Main       9.35 am    Bmouth Central    Main
 10.38 am Wareham       10.50 Main      11. 0 am      Wareham         Bay
  9. 4 am Souton T.     11.22 Main              (10.28 Wareham
 11.50 am Wareham       12.13 Main                arrd 10.54)
 12.40 pm       "        1. 3 Main      11.50 am     Wareham          Main
  1.15 pm       "        1.38 Main      12.40 pm        "             Main
  1.55 pm       "        2.18 Main       1.16 pm        "             Main
  2.42 pm       "        3. 6 Main       1.56 pm        "             Main
  4. 5 pm       "        4.28 Main       3.45 pm        "             Main
  1.17 pm Portsmth       5.13 Bay        4. 6 pm        "             Main
          (arr. 5.32)                    5.27 pm     Waterloo         Main
     (5.37 standing in Main with         6.35 pm        "             Main
      8 on, left 5.33).                   6.48 pm     Wareham         Main
  5.46 pm Wareham        6. 8 Bay         8. 6 pm        "             Main
          (arr. 6.17)                    8.38 pm     Eastleigh        Main
     (6.35 pm standing in Main           9.26 pm     Wareham         Main
      with 7 on)                         9.55 pm        "             Main
  6. 6 pm Wareham        6.28 Main
  8. 5 pm       "        8.28 Bay
     (8.38 pm standing in Main
      with 14-block set)
  9.34 pm Wareham        9.49 Main
 10.16 pm       "       10.38 Main
 11. 0 pm       "       11.34 Main
```

Operating procedure for August Bank Holiday 1933.

86. During the 1930s, in particular, many excursions from Bristol and Bath were worked via the Somerset & Dorset joint line, but the appearance of an LMS locomotive with one in July 1938 was most unusual. (S.C. Townrow)

87. Severe floods on 17th November 1935 made life particularly unpleasant for the shunter. In 1938, the canopy was rebuilt and lengthened at the same time as the rebuilding of the station offices. (Helen Muspratt)

1926

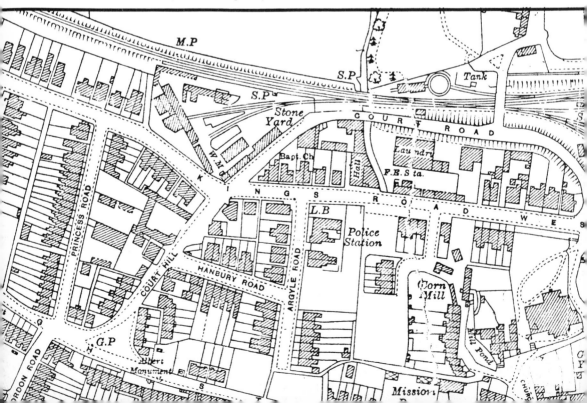

88. The fireman of class T1 no.7 catches up with his reading between the numerous reversals involved in shunting the yard on 19th July 1938. In the background is the back of the Congregational Chapel and the Parish Church; the crypt of the latter now houses the Swanage Model Railway Club. (J.G. Sturt)

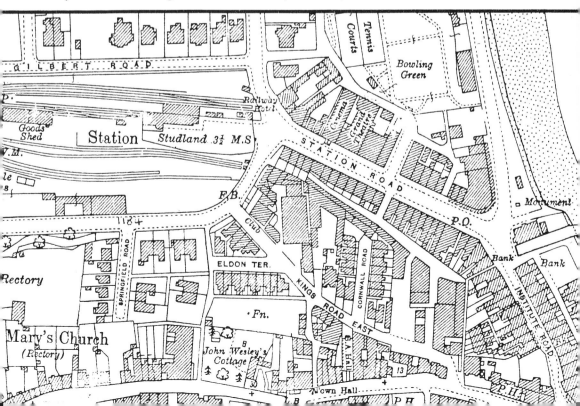

89. The station master's house on the right was retained almost unaltered when the station was rebuilt in 1938. The fluted "barley sugar" lamp posts unfortunately gave way to dull concrete ones during the SR modernisation programme. (Lens of Sutton)

90. The new platform canopy served an unexpected purpose during the fund raising "Salute the Soldier Week" in July 1944. John Wesley's cottage (shown on the earlier maps) was one of the buildings destroyed by German bombs. (W. Powell)

SWANAGE (BR)

91. Little changed with the formation of BR in 1948, the branch retaining its lovable unique characteristic. Two photographs taken on 9th September 1955 confirm this and show push-pull set no. 385 being shunted into the bay. Here, U class SR no. 1806 stands at the coal dock, with its BR prefix 3. (J.H. Aston)

LONDON & SOUTH WESTERN RAILWAY.

No. 016   Available from .... 19....

Issued subject to Conditions on other side.

NAME OF HOLDER. *Florence U Stiff*

SECOND CLASS SEASON TICKET

CORFE CASTLE & *Swanage*

Rate £1-17-6

AVAILABLE 3RD CLASS ONLY IF 2ND CLASS IS NOT PROVIDED

To expire ....

L·S·S·T·R·
TRESPASSERS
WILL BE
PROSECUTED

92. The starting signals were later put on a separate post, as shown in the next picture, and this former LSWR equipment was lost but the trespass warning sign remained for some time. (J.H. Aston)

94. Class 4 2–6–0 no. 76028 heads a through train in the main platform whilst M7 no. 30108 waits with a local service in the bay on 7th July 1963. The building by the coaches standing in no.4 siding is the former weighhouse and the flat roofed structure behind the signal box is an air-raid shelter. The window must have been added after the war. (C.L. Caddy)

93. A view from the buffer stops shows the uniform illumination achieved by the fully glazed canopy. The match-boarded coach on the right was added to the push-pull units when traffic increased. S10965 was built by the SR using two former SECR 6-wheeled coach bodies. (Lens of Sutton)

95. The SR used pre-cast concrete, reinforced with steel, for every possible application – platforms, fences, lamp posts and even signbaords. Sometimes the name was also cast in concrete but this one had an enamelled steel panel inserted in it. A juvenile railway photographer stands in the background. (C.L. Caddy)

97. An immaculate rebuilt West Country Pacific was undeniably an impressive sight, particularly on a short country branch line. *Crewkerne* leaves with one of the through Summer Saturday trains to Waterloo, that ran via Ringwood, in 1963. (C. Phillips)

96. The signal box was well positioned to give an excellent view of operations. An M7 is seen coming off shed in 1963. (C. Phillips)

99. No. 41238 takes water on the same day, alongside a growing heap of ash. The site was subsequently cleared and has now been restored, a replacement turntable being brought from Neasden in North London. (J. Scrace)

98. BR Standard class 4 no. 76013 shunts the yard on 11th June 1964. No.6 siding is in the foreground, no.1 being the bay road, not originally used for passengers. (J. Scrace)

100. Trains ancient and modern. A BR class 4 2–6–0 departs with two coaches at 5.57 for Wareham, whilst a Brush type 4 diesel-electric waits to leave at 6.12 for Eastleigh. This was the only through working on Sundays in the summer of 1964. (C. Phillips)

July 1924

		WAREHAM and SWANAGE.—Southern.							
Down.			**Week Days.**						**Sundays.**
M	Waterloo Station,	mrn	mrn	mrn	mrn	mrn	mrn	mrn	mrn		aft	aft	aft	aft	aft	aft	aft		mrn	mrn	aft
	156London...........dep.	....	....	5 40	....	5 50	8 30	10A30	1130	...	12B30	....	2J30	....	4 30	....	6 30	....	....	1130	2 0	...
—	Wareham ....dep.	8 0	9 10	9 46	1012	1137	12 4	1 24	2 35	...	3 24	4 35	5 24	6 2	7 29	8 10	9 23	...	1140	3 25	6 12	...
6	Corfe Castle............	8 13	9 23	9 59	1025	1150	1217	1 37	2 48	...	3 37	4 48	5 37	6 15	7 42	8 23	9 36	...	1153	3 38	6 25	...
11	Swanage ....arr.	8 26	9 37	1012	1038	12 1	1229	1 50	2 59	...	3 50	5 0	5 50	6 22	7 55	8 34	9 47	...	12 4	3 49	6 37	...
M	**Up.**	mrn|mrn| mrn |mrn|mrn|mrn|	aft	aft	aft	aft	aft	aft	aft	aft	aft		mrn	aft	aft
—	Swanage ....dep.	7 0	7 40	9 15	9 50	1050	1115	....	12 40	1 25	2 12	3 25	4 35	5 25	6 30	7 33	8 40	....	1015	2 30	5 15	...
5	Corfe Castle	7 11	7 51	9 28	10 1	11 1	1126	....	1251	3 8	2 23	3 36	4 46	5 36	6 41	7 44	8 51	...	1026	2 41	5 26	...
11	Wareham 156, 159...arr.	7 24	8 4	9 41	1017	1114	1139	....	1 4	3 50	2 36	9 50	5 4	5 50	6 54	7 58	9 4	...	1039	2 54	5 43	...
132	159London (Waterloo) arr.	....	11 0	124	50	2 15	....	2 50	....	4 50	6 21	6 55	....	8 50	1120	....	9 58	...	2 27	6 24	9 31	...
	A Leaves at 10 35 mrn. on Saturdays.			B Leaves at 12 35 aft. on Saturdays.						
	H Arrives at 12 56 aft. on Mondays and Saturdays.			J Leaves at 2 35 aft. on Saturdays.						

101. 1964 also saw the use of a set of Midland Region coaches, normally used on the Somerset & Dorset line. Smartly lined, their red livery made a pleasant change. (C. Phillips)

102. This is the same train, with no. 80085 blowing off ready to leave. The signal cannot be pulled off as the locomotive is standing past it and completing the track circuit. The signalman is therefore holding a green flag out of his window to authorise its departure. (C. Phillips)

103. Signalman Arthur Galton stands by the stove, whilst Shunter/Porter George Simms rests on the well-worn wooden lockers in the signal box. (C. Phillips)

104. The signalman has just caught the single-line token, as 2–6–2T no. 41320 drifts into the main platform in July 1965. Drivers in push-pull units had to leave their controls at this point to hand the tablet out of the window. The rules were altered to avoid this dangerous practice – they were allowed to keep it until the train had stopped and the fireman then had to walk to the signal box with it. (E. Wilmshurst)

105. Staff reductions were to be made with the introduction of DEMUs and the loco crew have "got the boot". They hold one up to emphasise the point. Curiously extra manpower was required to work the service with the otherwise efficient BR standard tanks, as they were not fitted for push-pull working. The shunting bell plunger on the roof stanchion was operated when the locomotive was ready to run round. (C. Phillips)

106. The 1938 building was tastefully carried out in Purbeck stone and blended well with the original station master's house beyond it. The window in the gable gave additional light to the booking hall. (D. Cullum)

107. By 1968, the Benn and Cronin Indicator looked neglected with many important destinations deleted and not even a poster in the centre panel. (D. Cullum)

108. Standard class 4 no. 80146 shunts on 27th August 1966 whilst another stands at the disused dock in no.3 siding. The goods yard had closed on 4th October 1965 but two roads were retained, for stabling purposes, until 6th June 1967 when the signal box also closed. (C.L. Caddy)

109. The arrival of a relief train from Waterloo hauled by D6507 was photographed on the same day. The ash heap has grown since we last saw it but would do so for only a few weeks longer. The shed doorway lost its elegant stone arch when an M7 over ran the turntable. (C.L. Caddy)

110. In 1967, the shed was derelict. Seldom photographed from this angle, this view shows the doorway at the west end and bridge 29 over the stream that runs through the town. The concrete hut is on the site of the siding that ran to the UDC yard until 1948. (D. Cullum)

111. The "basic railway" in August 1968, with the goods shed, air-raid shelter and weighbridge house standing redundant. The goods shed survived and the goods yard became a bus terminal and car park. (D. Cullum)

112. The twilight of BR operation. Despite strong protestations and numerous postponements of closure, the last trains ran on New Year's Day 1972. Unit no. 1110 was photographed that evening. (J.H. Bird)

4th October 1971 –
the last timetable issued

WAREHAM—SWANAGE
(Service liable to be withdrawn)

WEEKDAYS

									SX		SX	SO				
Waterloo 60 ...... dep.		1054	0830	....	1030	1230	1247	1430	1530	1447	1630	....	1830	....		
Southampton 60 ... dep.	0615	0716	0942	....	1142	1342	1416	1542	1642	1616	1742	....	1942	....		
Bournemouth 60 ... dep.	0630 0715	0800	1016	....	1216	1416	1500	1616	1725	1700	1816	....	2016	....		
Wareham .... dep.	0705 0816	0920	1052	....	1241	1445	1535	1644	1757	1757	1853	....	2043	....		
Corfe Castle	0716 0827	0931	1104	....	1252	1456	1546	1655	1808	1808	1904	....	2054	....		
Swanage	0725 0836	0939	1112	....	1301	1504	1555	1704	1817	1817	1913	....	2103	....		

SUNDAYS

	B		B	B		B	B
Waterloo 60 ...... dep.	1030	....	1230	1430	....	1630	1830
Southampton 60 .. dep.	1142	....	1342	1542	....	1742	1942
Bournemouth 60 .. dep.	1216	....	1416	1616	....	1816	2016
Wareham .... dep.	1242	....	1442	1642	....	1842	2045
Corfe Castle	1258	....	1458	1658	....	1858	2103
Swanage	1325	....	1518	1725	....	1936	2128

WEEKDAYS

	SX								SX	SO	SX				
Swanage	0630 0734	....	0854	0948	....	1145	....	1340	....	1510	1548	1616	1732	1820 1948	 2115
Corfe Castle	0639 0743	....	0903	0957	....	1154	....	1349	....	1519	1557	1625	1741	1829 1957	 2124
Wareham ...... arr.	0650 0754	....	0914	1008	....	1205	....	1400	....	1530	1608	1636	1752	1840 2008	 2135
Bournemouth 60 ... arr.	0723 0825	....	0950	1034	....	1234	....	1434	....	1634	1634	1750	1834	1950 2034	 2243
Southampton 60 ... arr.	0807 0909	....	1034	1109	....	1309	....	1509	....	1709	1709	1834	1909	2034 2109	 2334
Waterloo 60 ...... arr.	0923 1020	....	1204	1220	....	1421	....	1620	....	1823	1820	2004	2020	2204 2220	....

SUNDAYS

	B		B	B		B	B
Swanage	0930	....	1120	1330	....	1530	1710
Corfe Castle	0950	....	1147	1350	....	1550	1748
Wareham ...... arr.	1006	....	1203	1406	....	1606	1804
Bournemouth 60 ... arr.	1034	....	1234	1434	....	1634	1834
Southampton 60 ... arr.	1109	....	1309	1509	....	1709	1909
Waterloo 60 .... arr.	1220	....	1420	1620	....	1820	2020

B By Western National bus between Wareham & Swanage   SO Saturdays   SX Mondays to Fridays

113. After closure, every inch of rail was removed as far as Furzebrook sidings; only the stone structures remained standing. That could have been the end of the story had it not been for a group of determined railway enthusiasts (G.M. Moon)

FIRST LOCO
FOR
SWANAGE
RAILWAY

114. In 1975 the Swanage Railway Project obtained a licence for the use of the station buildings and the trackbed as far as the bridge in the previous picture. The Town Council had acquired the freehold from BR. With assistance from the Manpower Services Commission the missing portion of the canopy was replaced and the remainder renovated. The trackbed had to be dug out before relaying could commence. (J. Kellaway)

115. Morale was raised when the first locomotive was pushed into the former goods shed on 26th June 1976. It was *Beryl*, an 0–4–0 petrol locomotive from Corralls' coal depot at Poole. (J. Kellaway)

116. Work was well advanced in 1982 as a bulldozer starts to prepare the way for a run-round loop, whilst *Cunarder* simmers in the background. (D. Haysom)

117. An unexpected sight confronts Swanage shoppers on 22nd September 1976 as 2-6-4T no. 80078 is about to go against the traffic flow as it is reversed into the station yard. It had languished for ten years in a scrapyard at Barry. (J.Kellaway)

Stock list - February 1992

LOCOMOTIVES IN USE

1880	MR Class 1F 0-6-0T No.41708	(On loan from 1708 Trust)
1931	Hunslet 0-6-0T No.1690 Cunarder	(On loan from 1708 Trust)
1899	LSWR Class T9 4-4-0 No. 30120	(On loan from National Rail Museum)
1951	LNER Class J72 0-6-0T No.69023	(On hire from N.E.L.P.G.).
1960	Yugo USA Class 0-6-0T No.30075	(Owned by members of Swanage Railway)

LOCOMOTIVES UNDERGOING RESTORATION

1905   LSWR Class M7 0-4-4T No.35053
(Owned by Drummond Locomotive Society. Restoration at Chappel , Essex).
1954   BR Standard Class 4MT 2-6-4T No.80078
(Owned by 80078 Owners group. Restoration at Swanage).
1954   BR Standard Class 4MT 2-6-4T No.80104
(Owned by 80104 Co.Ltd., Restoration at Bitton, Avon).
1928   GWR 0-6-2T No.6695
(Private owner. Restoration at Swanage).

LOCOMOTIVES AWAITING RESTORATION

1948   SR 'Merchant Navy' Class 4-6-2 No.35022 Holland America Line.
(Owned by SST. Stored at Swanage).
1954   Peckett Class OQ 0-6-0ST No.2150
(Private owner. Stored at Swanage).
1930   Hunslet 0-4-0T No.1684
(Private owner. Stored at Swanage).

DIESEL LOCOMOTIVES IN USE

1958	BR 350 hp No.D3591 (08 476)
1964	BR 450 hp No.D9521 (NCB NO.3 ; Class 14)

LOCOMOTIVES NOT IN USE

1937   Hibberd 'Planet' 4 Wheel Petrol Mechanical 'Beryl'
(Privately owned).
1957   Fowler 0-4-0 Diesel Mechanical No.4210132 'May'
(Privately owned).

CARRIAGES IN USE

1956	-	Mk.1 TSO	No.4416
1956	-	Mk.1 TSO	No.4349
1957	-	Mk.1 SO	No.4803
1961	-	Mk.1 RMB	No.1874
1957	-	Mk.1 RU	No.1908
1951	-	Mk.1 SKH	No.24127
1957	-	Mk.1 SK	No.25424
1955	-	Mk.1 BSOB	No.9015
1956	-	Mk.1 BSK	No.35059
1958	-	Mk.1 BCK	No.21205
1958	-	MK.1 SLS	No.2564
1947	-	Bulleid CK	No.5761

CARRIAGES OUT OF USE

1930	-	Maunsell TO	No.1381
1947	-	Bulleid BTSO	No.4365

COACHES UNDERGOING RESTORATION

1959	-	Mk.1 FO	No.3090
1953	-	Mk.1 RMB	No.1885

UNRESTORED COACHES

1956	-	Mk.1 CK	No.7673
1956	-	Mk.1 TSO	No.4055
1956	-	Mk.1 TSO	No.4074
1947	-	Bulleid TO	No.1457
1947	-	Bulleid BTSO	No.4366
1935	-	Maunsell BDT	No.6699

118. In 1980, it was again possible to travel behind a steam locomotive to Swanage, albeit only over a very short distance. This is the Andrew Barclay 0–4–0ST *Richard Trevithick*, which was later transferred to the Swindon & Cricklade Railway. (J. Kellaway)

119. The sceptics have been confounded by the unimaginable transformation of the site. Hawthorn Leslie 0–6–0ST *Linda* (ex-Corby Iron & Steel Works) departs at 14.00 on 3rd May 1986 for the 25 minute return journey. A Gloucester DMU set stands outside the goods shed, which is used as a workshop. The water tank is from Barry Dock station and the boiler is from Hunslet 0–6–0ST *Cunarder*. The track panels were acquired from the Isle of Grain and are for use in the track restoration towards Corfe Castle. (V. Mitchell)

120. *Linda* arrives at the 1986 limit of operations, Herston Halt, on 11th May. The rear coach is former SR "Brighton Belle" Pullman car no. 88, complete with its driving compartment which is now used by the guard. (D. Morgan)

HERE IS THE NEWS .... on 7th March 1992 ....

It is a 20 year old dream come true for the volunteers who started rebuilding the old branch line from a disused station site at Swanage back in 1976.

From Corfe Castle, it is just one and a half miles to the BR network between Furzebrook and Norden. After the last BR train ran down to Corfe Castle and Swanage on New Year's Day 1972, the six and a half miles of track between Swanage, Corfe and Norden was ripped up for scrap.

Although they did not realise at the time, when early Swanage Railway campaigners paid £500 to British Rail back in 1972 not to take up the valuable stone ballast along with the tracks, they were saving the modern Swanage Railway hundreds of thousands of pounds and months of extra work.

Since volunteers started relaying the Purbeck Line from nothing back in 1976, they have laid over 2,500 tonnes of track

- 900 rails, 11,000 wooden and concrete sleepers, and gone through over 70,000 bolts and 22,000 heavy iron track chairs. After reaching the site of Norden Halt, the volunteers will be returning to Corfe Castle to relay the 12-coach passing loop and then a second siding into the goods yard at the restored Victorian station. Plans are being made for services to be restored to Corfe Castle and Norden early in 1993.

A remarkable 20 year old dream finally comes true as elated Swanage Railway volunteers begin to relay the final one and a half mile link of track between Corfe Castle and the BR network at Furzebrook.

An important piece of British railway history is being made against the dramatic backcloth of Corfe Castle's Medieval ruins with the Swanage Railway relaying the final link between the Purbeck Line and the BR system.

121. A three-mile journey to Harmans Cross became possible on 4th March 1989 when this station was reopened. A number of locomotives from other preserved lines have visited the line. These have included two 0-6-0PTs, ex-GWR 0-6-2T no. 5619 and 4-6-2 no. 34072 *257 Squadron*. This is ex-LNER 0-6-2T no. 69621 from Chappel & Wakes Colne in Essex and is seen on 8th July 1990. (T.Wright)